ROMAN EMPIRE
Copyright © 2023 Samuel John

ACCORDING TO LEGEND, ROME WAS FOUNDED BY TWO TWIN BROTHERS RAISED BY A SHE-WOLF.

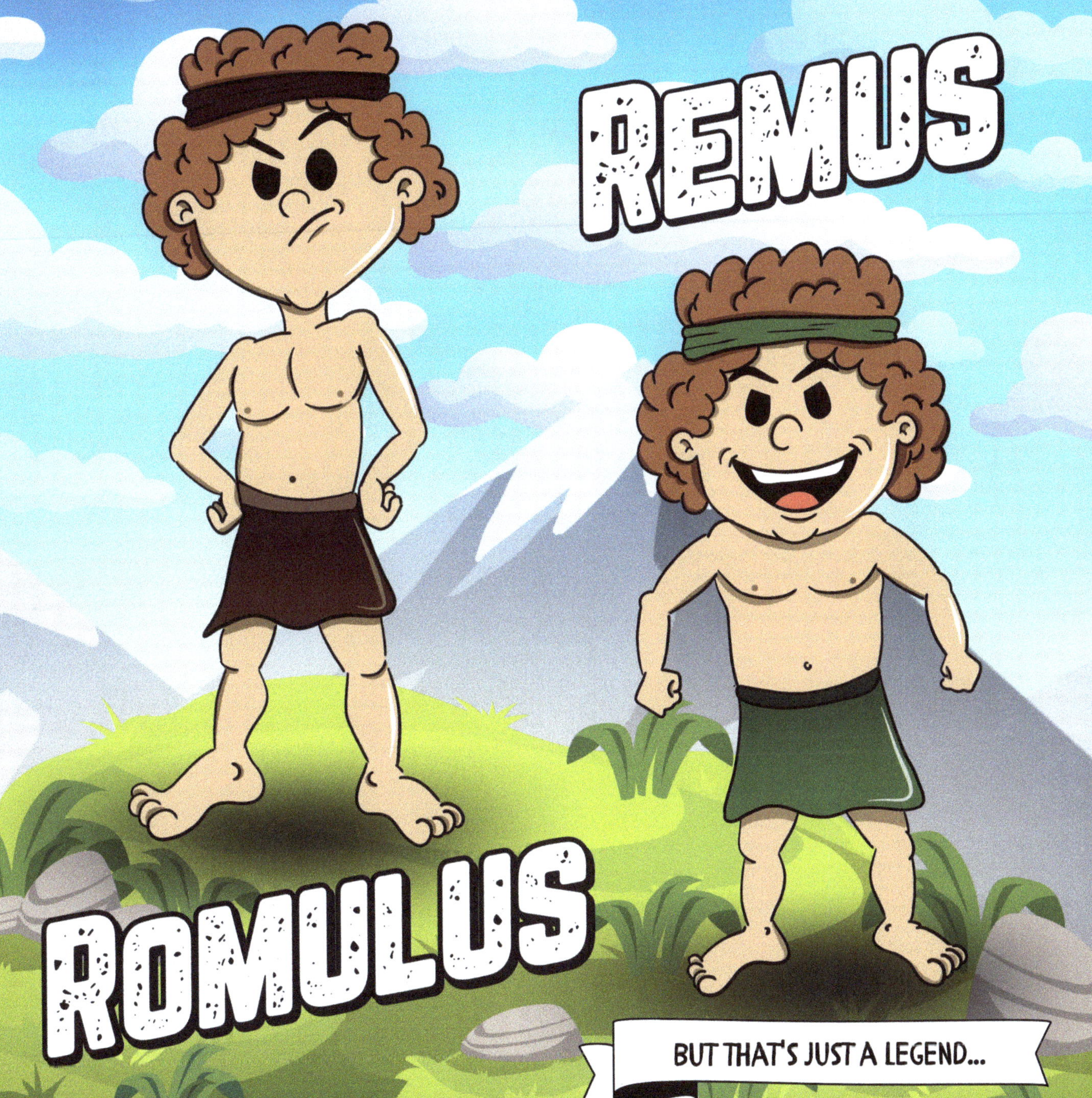

REMUS
ROMULUS
BUT THAT'S JUST A LEGEND...

ACTUALLY, ROME WAS FOUNDED AFTER THE UNION OF SEVERAL VILLAGES LOCATED ON THE BANKS OF THE TIBER RIVER, IN WHAT WE KNOW TODAY AS ITALY.

That was around
753 B.C.

Almost 2,800
years ago!

AT THE BEGINNING, ROME WAS A MONARCHY RULED BY 7 KINGS:

ROMULUS

NUMA POMPILIUS

TULLUS HOSTILIUS

ANCUS MARCIUS

TARQUINIUS PRISCUS

SERVIUS TULLIUS

TARQUINIUS SUPERBUS

THE FACT THAT THE FIRST KING OF ALL WAS ROMULUS MAKES US THINK THAT THIS STAGE OF THE HISTORY OF ROME IS A MIXTURE OF TRUTH AND LEGEND.

LATER A REPUBLIC WAS ESTABLISHED. THIS WAS A FORM OF GOVERNMENT IN WHICH THERE WERE NO KINGS, BUT POLITICIANS WERE IN CHARGE OF MAKING DECISIONS.

THE ROMAN REPUBLIC LASTED FOR SEVERAL CENTURIES, UNTIL THE STAGE WE KNOW TODAY AS THE ROMAN EMPIRE BEGAN.

ROMAN EMPIRE

IN THIS MODEL OF GOVERNMENT, THE EMPEROR HAD ALL THE POWER AND WAS THE ONE WHO MADE THE DECISIONS, ALTHOUGH HE WAS ADVISED BY A SENATE.

THE ROMAN EMPIRE OCCUPIED TERRITORIES THROUGHOUT THE MEDITERRANEAN, ENCOMPASSING THE THREE CONTINENTS KNOWN AT THE TIME: AFRICA, EUROPE, AND ASIA.
SPQR

AMONG THE LANDS CONQUERED WERE BRITAIN, HISPANIA, GREECE, EGYPT, GAUL, GERMANIA AND NORTH AFRICA.

ROMAN SOCIETY

PATRICIANS

- This was the group with the most power and wealth.
- They were aristocratic families that provided the empire's political, religious, and military leadership.
- They were free and had rights and privileges.

PLEBEIANS

- Plebeians were average working citizens of Rome: farmers, bakers, builders or craftsmen.
- Although they were free and had rights, they did not enjoy the same privileges as the patricians. They could not govern and had to pay taxes.

SLAVES

- They were prisoners of war or children of slaves.
- They were not free and had no rights.
- They were the property of their masters and of the Roman Empire.
- They could be sold or bought as objects.

THE ANCIENT ROMANS WERE EXCELLENT ARCHITECTS. THEY BUILT WALLED CITIES, IN WHICH THERE WAS NO LACK OF ALL KINDS OF PUBLIC BUILDINGS FOR VARIOUS SERVICES AND ACTIVITIES.

THERE WERE THEATERS, FORUMS, AMPHITHEATERS, CIRCUSES, THERMAL BATHS... AND EVEN SCHOOLS FOR CHILDREN!

Roman Colosseum
(Flavian Amphitheatre)

PUBLIC SPECTACLES, SUCH AS GLADIATORIAL COMBATS, WERE HELD IN THE AMPHITHEATERS.

Aqueduct of Segovia

THANKS TO THE AQUEDUCTS, THE ROMANS WERE ABLE TO TRANSPORT WATER TO ALL THE CITIES OF THE EMPIRE.

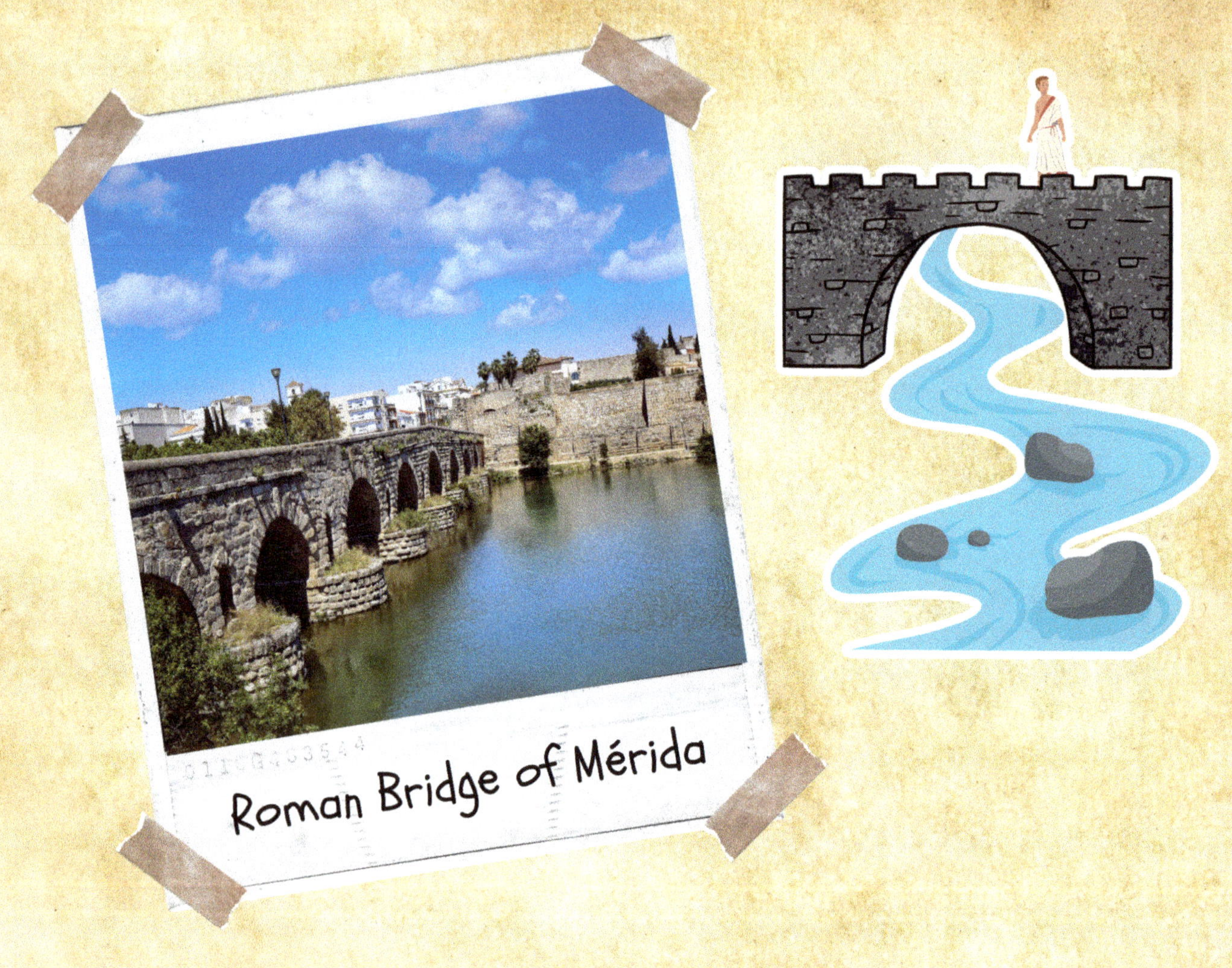

Roman Bridge of Mérida

THE ROMANS WERE THE FIRST TO BUILD LARGE, LONG-LASTING BRIDGES. THEY WERE USED TO CROSS THE WATER AND CONTINUE ALONG THE SAME PATH.

Roman Theatre of Mérida

CLASSICAL PLAYS WERE PERFORMED IN THE ROMAN THEATER. IT WAS ONE OF THE MOST IMPORTANT BUILDINGS IN LARGE CITIES.

THE ROMANS BUILT ROADS THAT CONNECTED ALL PARTS OF THE EMPIRE. THEY WERE THE EQUIVALENT OF TODAY'S ROAD NETWORK.

Do you know the expression "all roads lead to Rome"?

Well, that's where it originated. At that time, all the roads in the Empire led to Rome.

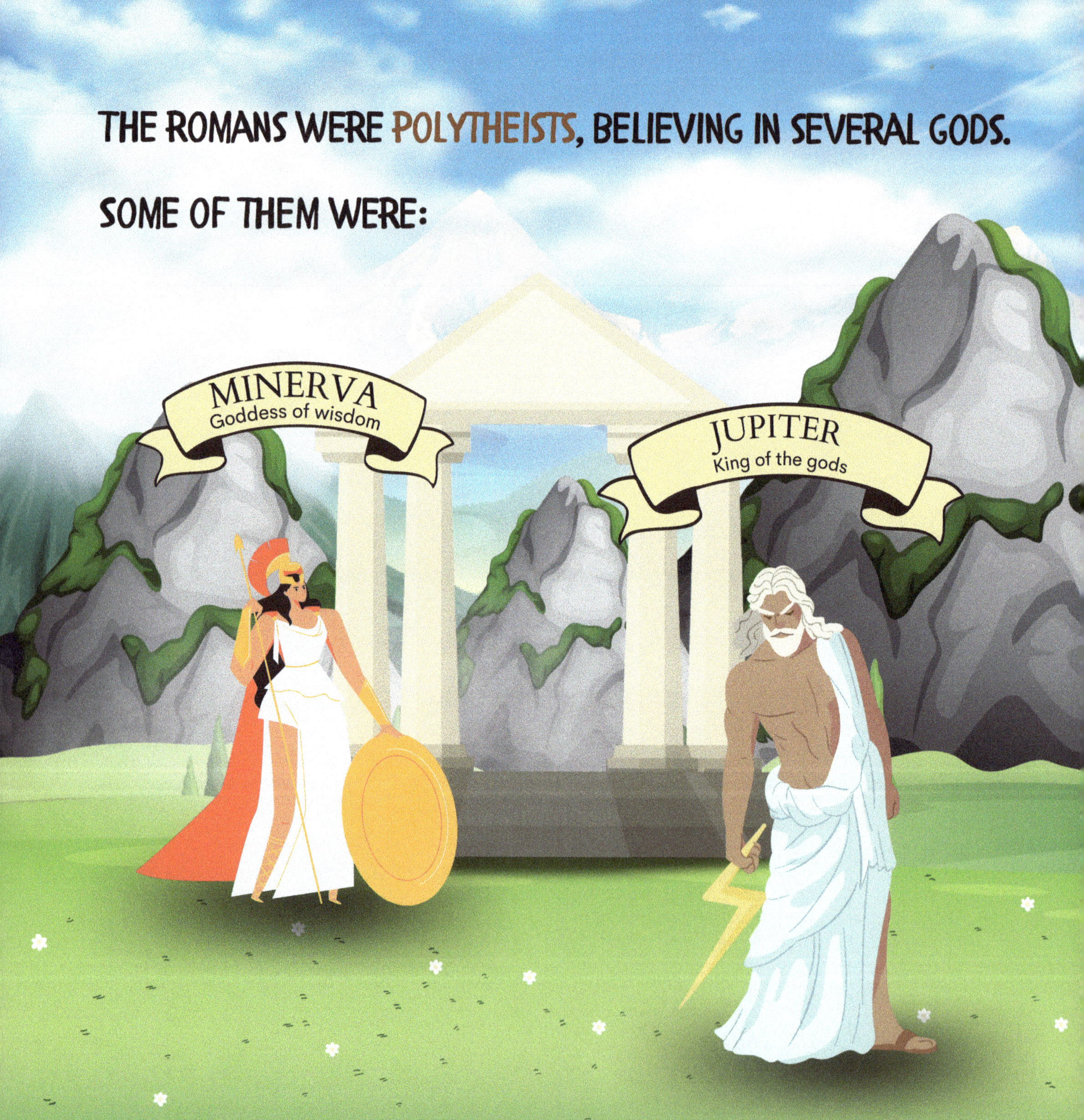

THE ROMANS WERE POLYTHEISTS, BELIEVING IN SEVERAL GODS.

SOME OF THEM WERE:

MINERVA
Goddess of wisdom

JUPITER
King of the gods

NEPTUNE
God of sea and oceans
MARS
God of war
VENUS
Goddess of love

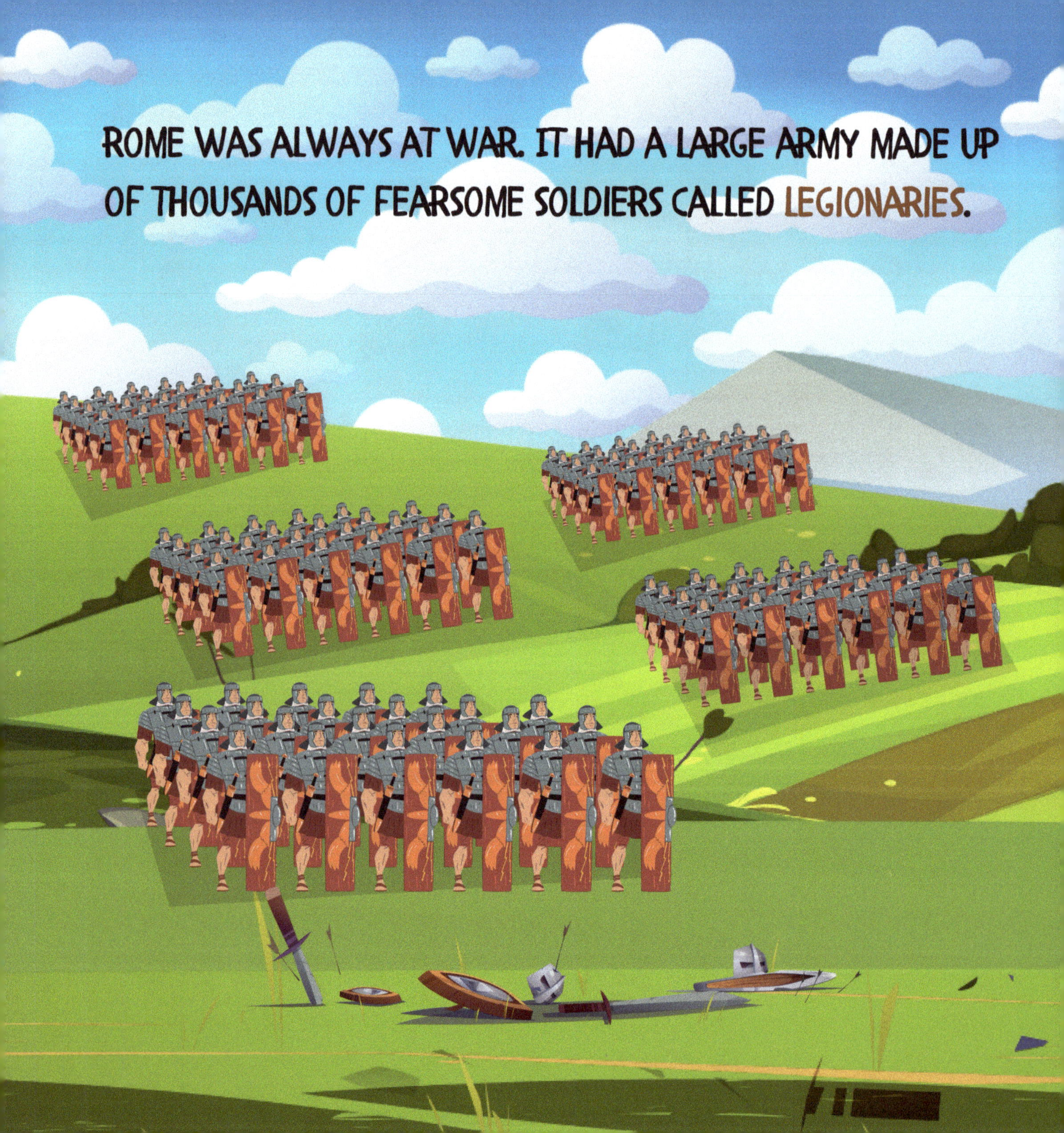

ROME WAS ALWAYS AT WAR. IT HAD A LARGE ARMY MADE UP
OF THOUSANDS OF FEARSOME SOLDIERS CALLED LEGIONARIES.

THE LEGIONARIES WERE VERY WELL TRAINED. THANKS TO THEM AND THEIR EFFECTIVE COMBAT STRATEGIES, THE CONQUEST OF NEW TERRITORIES WAS ACHIEVED.

IN THE 5TH CENTURY, THE ROMAN EMPIRE FELL DUE TO THE INVASIONS OF THE GERMANIC PEOPLES.

TODAY WE ARE STILL INFLUENCED BY EVERYTHING THAT THOSE ANCIENT ROMANS LEFT US. THIS CAN BE SEEN IN THE CULTURE, POLITICS, ART, LAWS, THE CALENDAR, THE ORGANIZATION OF THE CITIES, ETC.

And here it ends! I hope you liked it and learned new things.

I want to ask you a favor so that this book reaches more people, and that is that you rate it with a sincere opinion on the platform where you purchased it.

With that small gesture, you will be helping me to carry on with new projects.

I can't wait to start creating
my next book for you!

See you soon!

KEEP LEARNING WITH OUR EDUCATIONAL CHILDREN'S BOOKS

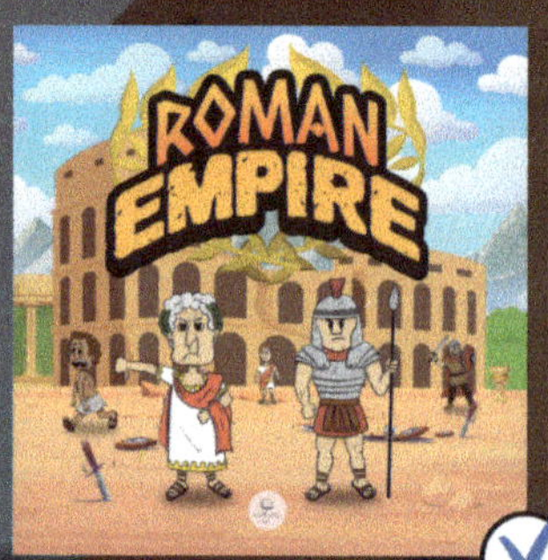

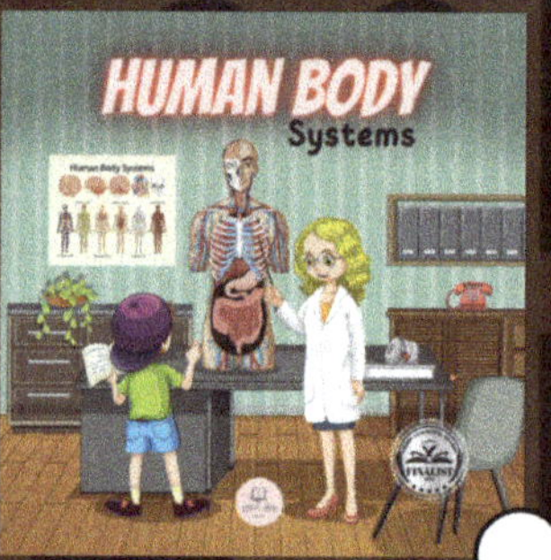

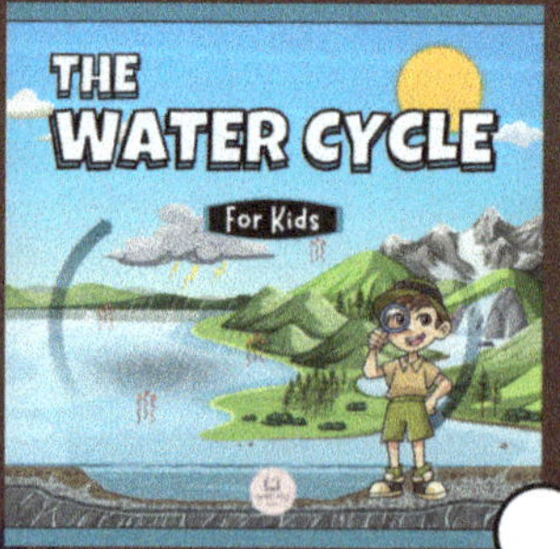

https://www.pge.me/childrensbooks

Subscribe to my newsletter and stay informed of new publications, offers and free book promotions.

www.subscribepage.io/ebookfree

FOLLOW ME

www.amazon.com/author/samueljohnbooks

The Steadfast
Tin Soldier
SCAN ME
www.azonlinks.com/841269984X
SAMMIE EXPLORES
THE SOLAR SYSTEM
Ages 3-6
SCAN ME
www.azonlinks.com/8412699866